ABOUT THE AUTHOR

John Walker-Smith is an Australian with dual
British citizenship. He is a medical graduate of the
University of Sydney and is now Emeritus Professor
of Paediatric Gastroenterology University of
London. He has lived in London since 1973.

His wife died from Alzheimer's disease in 2019. He has
two living children and eight grandchildren. His second
daughter tragically died aged 29 years in 2004. This was
followed by the death of his nephew aged 33 years.
These events led him to write poetry for the first time.

He has an MA in Christianity and the Arts at
King's College London. He is a member of The
King's Chapel of the Savoy. He is Life President
of the Crohn's in Childhood Research Appeal
and the Founder President of CAPGAN.

John Angus Walker-Smith

HOPE, BEAUTY AND FRIENDSHIP

AUSTIN MACAULEY PUBLISHERS™

LONDON • CAMBRIDGE • NEW YORK • SHARJAH

A CIP catalogue record for this title is available from the British Library.

ISBN 9781035833887 (Paperback)
ISBN 9781035833894 (Hardback)
ISBN 9781035833917 (ePub e-book)
ISBN 9781035833900 (Audiobook)

www.austinmacauley.com

First Published 2023
Austin Macauley Publishers Ltd
1 Canada Square
Canary Wharf
London
E14 5AA

DEDICATION

In loving memory of my beloved
daughter, Laura (1975–2004)

ACKNOWLEDGEMENTS

Both family and friends have helped in this
endeavour over a number of years, in various
ways. My daughter Louise typed the complete
manuscript. Zoe Rucker was a very valuable critic of
my individual poems. Ian McNaught Davis sustained
me when I worried about the worth of my poems

I thank many friends over a lifetime, who
have inspired my appreciation of their various
friendships, some of them across the world.
Several of them are now departed this life.

INTRODUCTION

I had never written any poetry until the tragic death of my daughter Laura. However, this triggered a series of poems related to loss and "after loss". I then began to look back on my childhood and my family events, etc., and wrote some poems on these themes.

Most of the subsequent poems related to contemporary events that I experienced in my family and beyond. Certain themes emerged, including poems about war and terror, as well as more benign topics such as royalty and the medical life, based on my own experiences. The pandemic with the lockdowns were a further powerful stimulus to write poems related to that theme. More recently, the Ukraine War and the death of Queen Elizabeth were further triggers to poems.

The theme of friendship has been very important over many years, right up to the present time. However, I now realize that the theme of my hope to see Laura again in the life eternal was the unconscious background to many poems. The concept of transcendental beauty arose in my latter metaphysical poems, vide 'Roman Glass' and 'The Colour Blue'. I encountered in these poems the concept of transcendental beauty.

I believe every reader will react to individual poems in a uniquely personal way, in the context of their own experiences

I have chosen free verse as my poetic style, following the example of T S Eliot. I hope there is hint of rhythm in every poem.

JOHN ANGUS WALKER-SMITH
Chingford, Essex, UK
April 2023

POEMS

LOSS AND AFTER

1. Loss

Choosing to go, you I cannot summon back,
Yet I store the hours we spent together,
Walking the shore in Bondi's winter
Till erasing that fell day, I almost believe
I shall see you home again once more,
Sometimes, I glimpse you amidst the throng,
Or fashion-loving gallery crowd
So sad it is that we shall walk no more,
But I yearn for that eternal day,
On another shore, when together shall we be.

2. Butterfly

My butterfly you
Soared upwards to the sky,
But reality was harsh,
So down, down you came,
Desolate when he had gone.
O my butterfly.
So ephemeral,
So short the time with us
But your beauty shines with light
Golden wings with opals bedecked.

3. The Wedding

The bells rang, you asked for whom,
With veil upon your face, you turned,
Side by side we walked.
These last minutes you were mine
Soon you will be forever his.
Sadness and joy flowed together,
As the organ sounded and the bells rang,
My daughter now a woman, complete,
Walks with him along the aisle,
With happiness for all to see.

The day my daughter married,
Bridesmaids two had she.
My second daughter and my niece, they were,
Behind you down the aisle they went.
My second daughter with flowers bedecked,
Like a Grecian maid was she.
My niece with blossoming beauty
From far away had come.
A cornucopia of life has flowed, from bride and niece,
But not from my Grecian maid.

My hope beside her, up the aisle to walk,
Was thwarted by another choice she made.
But O, how I wish that day had come.

4. Butterflies

How long do they last?
Butterflies, butterflies,
Where do they go?

Butterflies, butterflies,
May soon disappear,
When they are gone,
What may remain?

Memories, memories
Which often retain,
A hope for love,
Which reality
Could not sustain.

5. Spring

In Woodford Green
Now, the light of hope,
Shines into the house of grief,
As spring lightens our lives
With its Easter brilliance,
Bright and clear.

In April, yellow, white and gold,
Amidst the dazzling green,
Lift our hearts.

In May, bluebells and forget-me-nots
Within the darkening green
Delight us.

In the woods of Wanstead Park,
The youthful sycamores
Among the ancient oaks,
Tell us of new life arising,
Amidst the old,
As I and grandson dear,
Walk together.

Nearby in St Mary's Churchyard
Frolicsome forget-me-nots
Remind us,
Of the "Love that wilt not let thee go".
Dad and nephew stand below,
The ancient yew,
And remember thee.

6. Love Remembered: Two Years On

Together they lie.
Berries of holly,
Leaves of gum tree,
Intertwined,
Amidst the autumn gold.

Together we stand,
Intertwined,
Remembering you,
But you are not there.

Yet the memory,
It is strong,
Here in this sacred place.

Your love,
Our love,
We will never let go.

7. My Nephew

He is dead!
The cry goes out.
He is dead.
It cannot be so.

Is the young man gone?
Yes.
But he did not choose to go.

Lamentation upon lamentation.
"Thou has removed my soul,
Far off from peace."

Yet
"Have I hope",
Even in the midst of loss.
So very great.
Lord,
With us abide.

8. Funeral Days

Once more a house of grief,
Wet and cold,
In Lindfield again,
Once more a funeral for youth and beauty.

33 years was all he had,
But our Lord had no more.
For me his life alone
Keeps the flame of hope alive.

Are the cousins together now,
On another shore?
My hope can only be,
That this is so.

Both lives were rich in love,
Given and received.
Much love flowed out,
On their funeral days.

9. Her Birthday

This silence I must bear,
To live alone; I did not choose.
This burden I must bear.

Your voice has gone: forever.
But today I think of you.

Born with beauty, sweet,
Thirty years and more
So long ago.

O daughter dear,
In the silence,
With joy,
I remember you.

10. Motet: O Lord My Hope and Strength

O lord my hope and strength
In my desolation, I turned to you.
A knife had pierced my heart.
It was to occur once more.

Long was the night of my despair.
But you were there for me.
I put my trust in you.
You gave me strength to journey on.

The mark of Cain seemed on my brow,
But you sent my friends to comfort me.
I rose on eagle wings.
I did not faint.

How beautiful is your Holiness, O Lord,
The earth is filled with your glory.

*Set to choral music by Philip Berg, performed
several times by choir of Savoy Chapel*

11. Time and Memory

Wandering in the gallery
Hoping to come upon
Memories, instead I found
The paintings, they had gone!

With a sob, involuntary,
My chest was filled,
My heart cried out,
Crivelli, where are you?

Time breaks the thread of memory.
Things pass and time goes on.
O memories stay, I pray,
For her, I have loved so well.

She chose to go,
Despite her beauty fair,
Plain to all who knew her,
And so very clear to me.

Crivelli, you have taught me,
Such beauty is so real.
And Heaven too, you show,
For us it is not so far away.

You reveal to us,
Timeless in their beauty,
Loving mother with beauteous babe,
And saints in Heaven too.

Sebastian with beautiful serenity,
Reveals the reward of faith.
He shows us hope,
To calm our fears.

Time must onward go.
The years pass so fast.
Sweet memories are a blessing,
For calming our distress.

The paintings they are gone.
This fills me with such loss.
Images do trigger hope,
But all cannot be lost.

Calm comes over me,
As I walk away.
Loss cannot dictate
The pains of day to day.

Loss of images, so fair,
Cannot the thread of memories break.
Time alone can do it,
As life itself, must pass away.

Yet while life remains a blessing,
And time onward goes,
Sweet memories may sustain us,
Although images may go.

FAMILY

12. My Wife

Glistening in the sun, your golden hair,
Framed your youthful face,
With all its brightness and hope.
Upon the beach you rested,
After the cold sea.
This land of sun and beauty had given you,
A new liberty for life and love.
So lucky me to find,
This Scottish lass in this Southern land
So far from home and yet at home for me.

13. Goodbye

It is fifty years, since I my troth did plight
To thee, O best beloved.
Years have come and gone.

It was the spring of our delight,
When from our tree burst forth, the buds of spring.
Summer came, the flowers did bloom.
But one did fall away.

The days lengthened, as autumn fell,
Then bleak winter came.
Black clouds did overcome thee.

But the pipes did sing on your funeral day.
And our bairns live on.

Goodbye. Goodbye.

14. Our Son

Unto us a child was born.
You were the son indeed.
The longed-for one,
Who family name would bear.
Upon your shoulder would this a burden be?
But freedom would be yours,
And freedom comes like love,
With time, experience and life.
You tiny babe, bound with love,
We speed you on to many a happy day.

15. My Sister

At Euston you were waiting
From Liverpool I had come.
First journey, underground,
Earl's Court was our port of call,
First port for Aussies coming "home".
Next was Piccadilly and its lights.
Onwards in the morning,
Scotland was our goal,
To Mull's beauteous isle,
Whence Dad's forbears had come.
She and I, together,
So much, to enjoy and share,
As we travelled around the land.
The land from whence we had "come".
Strengthened was my fraternal love,
Growing from earliest years.

16. My Cousin

Handsome and brave, he served his King
And died to keep Australia free.
Across the Coral Sea, his plane he flew,
Until from out of sunset,
The enemy planes did come.
These he could not see.
His life was snatched from him,
So full of life and young.
Each Anzac Day a little cross.
My grandmother would place,
Upon the remembrance field,
With tears her pain expressed.

17. The Day My Mother Died

My mother in the arms of Jesus,
So my dream revealed.
She left that day,
With a speed that passed belief,
But belief she had,
With a deep, deep faith in God.

The day my mother died,
My father pushed me away.
I understood the pain and grief,
That he suffered on that day.
But I was suffering too.
The stiff upper lip was his lifetime code.
Otherwise, on that fell day,
It could not be.

Later, as years flowed on,
And children came there more,
He mellowed and could reveal
His "milk of human kindness".
It was his real way.
Then both of us could share,
The loss we had together,
The day my mother passed away.

TERROR AND WAR

18. Tavistock Square

You cruel man, you cruel man,
How could you kill them all?
The doctors come; the doctors come.
The blood is on the wall.
Once more the square is terror-struck,
Once more the people flee.
So many years, O London,
Since bombs rained down on thee.
When will all human hearts disclaim,
Such wickedness and sin,
And love and truth reclaim?

Around the altar, all you stood,
The lady priest the words of Jesus read,
And gave you each the symbol of his blood.
Outside the blood had spilled,
From many loved by you.
What unimaginable pain to bear,
But He it is who on the cross
Can grief assuage.
Love and hope, through Him,
Can turn much hate to love.

Amidst the many flowers and words,
Upon the church's steps,
One message caught my eye.
With love from Kuwait, it said.
From that Arab land for which our lads had fought,
Came greetings at this terrible time.
It made me feel that, in the end,
Love can triumph still.

19. Death and Resurrection in Dresden

O Frauenkirche,
O Frauenkirche,
How terrible was your fall.
The firestorm destroyed you.
The innocent many
And the guilty few,
Alike,
Died together,
On that so terrible night.

O Frauenkirche,
O Frauenkirche,
Now wonderfully restored,
By peace and reconciliation,
Your glory shines once more,
Crowned with golden orb and cross
Above,
And Luther at the door
Below.

But the memory is forever,
Of those who died in war,
In Coventry and Dresden,
And many cities more.

A new peace there is in Europe,
But war goes on elsewhere.
Yet your resurrection from the ruins,
So long after your fall,
Symbolises our hope and prayer,
That the Lord of Peace Himself
Will give us enduring peace
Once more.
That peace which passes all understanding.

20. Twenty Thousand to Go

Three thousand dead!
Old men send young men to war!
It has ever been so.

Young Americans dying,
So far from home.
Why do they die?

Is it for King and Country?
No, it is for democracy,
They say.

Democracy,
What is that?
Said the Athenian slave.

Democracy,
What is that?
Said the Ulster Unionist.

What is that?
Said the Iraqi mother,
Cradling her dying son.

What is that?
Said the American mom,
As she mourns her son.

Her son whose blood
Mingles with those
He killed.

War, war, war,
The heart despairs.
When will they learn?

When will they learn?
Learn of that love
That passes all understanding.

21. Names upon the Wall

Rugby memorial chapel,
The names are on the wall.
Translucent in the window,
Shines forth above us all,
Upon the cross, our Lord.

Those names, those names,
To Him alone are known,
Though life has fled, yet
Our hope and prayer it is,
Those names, with Him,
Do stand upon another shore.

Yet what a loss for England,
Those names, upon the wall.
Sons and daughters, so very few,
When they passed away,
Too young, too fair,
To die upon a foreign field,
A field, so very, very,
Far away, from home.

As the sound of music,
Both played and said,
Rose to the celestial vault,
Inspired by you, O Rupert,
With your name upon the wall,
Our thoughts did turn
To clouds, to waves,
To cool flowers,
And white cups and plates,
Upon the wall.

Yet in other parts of England,
New names go on the wall.
Though nigh a hundred year have passed,
The loss of youth goes on.

When will this gentle land,
This sweet land,
A land
Of friends and laughter,
Be at peace for evermore,
With no new names from foreign field,
To go upon the wall?

And in that foreign field,
In that Afghan land,
So very far away,
Nigh two hundred names,
And more,
Now are on the wall.
They join those names,
So long ago,
Of countrymen who died,
In far-off times,
So far from this sweet land.

When, oh when,
The cry goes out,
Will Man
Such killings
Cause to cease?

22. Osler and Son

Where now I am,
Revere with father,
Here did stand,
Army clad,
So tall, severe.

Now
A hundred years on,
Reflect do I,
Upon the love they shared,
So long ago.

Such love, so deep,
And yet not for man to see,
By death, asunder was it cut,
On Flanders Field,
So very far away.

But can love ever die?
No,
But love does change,
And be transformed.

It is my belief and hope
That on another shore,
Father and son,
Now, today,
Together are.

This will then
Be seen by all,
Arising from their graves
On Resurrection Day,
Love triumphant in the end.

23. Suffer Little Children

Children dead on the road,
Shrapnel in legs of babies,
Holy innocents,
Beloved by God,
Jesus saith, *Come unto me.*

Guided by mothers,
Children struggling to escape,
Satanic powers reducing
This God-given land
To a living hell.

Mother and child, sacred duo,
The holiest of images,
On the train they go,
But where to?
They do not know.

Fathers alone,
Desolation in grief,
Left to fight evil destruction
Of this fertile land.

Long-suffering Ukraine,
Where Stalin starved the land,
Now Putin invades,
A land waylaid
By Satan's power,
Bombing hospitals,
The land and its people.

But love and care still remain
In the land of the Ukraine,
Now a land of pain.
Warriors risk their lives
Yet have time to aid
The infirm and the afflicted.
Humanity still is here
In this besieged land
Where cruelty has come,
But can love withstand?

Death and destruction
Onward go.
Is a just peace just a dream?

The cry goes out,
When, O when
Will killing innocents cease?

MEDICINE

24. Consultant and Child

They called me in the early hours:
Should they let you go?
Death was close, they told me.
Germs were in your blood,
Your diagnosis uncertain.
It would be the kindest thing.
No, I said to them,
There is a chance, fight for his life.
Weeks later finally we diagnosed
Autoimmune enteropathy,
A strange name to say,
A disorder new,
But once we had an answer,
Treatment there came,
And after many years now
A fine young man you are.
I am so glad that no was my answer.

25. Grandson

Eight days old and a life at risk!
Locally admitted, a difficult time.
Confusion and uncertainty reigned.
My daughter distraught, myself distressed.
But a telephone call to Hackney Road,
And soon he was in the Queens.
Calm and order quickly came,
The surgeon was in charge.
She rapidly solved and discovered
The medical way to go,
Amidst the archaic buildings,
And the crumbling Victorian façade.

Modern science and teamwork succeeded,
But Bottomley's will prevailed,
And those medical teams are long gone,
Split and dispersed by government decree.
Thank God, they were there for our grandson,
On that blessed day when calm prevailed,
And wisdom showed the way.
Now he is a healthy lad, with a life ahead,
But another outcome there could have been,
If he had not made the journey to Hackney Road.

26. Closing Casualty

Some ten years ago or more,
Casualties were closing,
Right across London Town.
Barts at first and the Queens,
And many, many more.
The other night,
My daughter with my grandson,
To the local casualty, we went.
The facilities were modern,
But the waiting area quite unkempt.
Waited, we waited from 9 till 5am,
The doctors, few, were very good,
But O, there was too much to do.
Now of London's casualties,
There are far too few,
And the loss of Queens is mourned still
By the kids of London's East End.

27. A Lamentation

On the occasion of admission to a medical ward 2016

Where are all the English nurses? Where have they
gone?
Cheerful Filipino girls are here, with all their little
kindnesses.
Smooth Romanians glide about the ward. Caribbean
girls are here.
Tall African male nurses striding along the wards, with
their long legs.

Where are all the English nurses, where have they
gone?
Italians are here, happily singing as they cross the
ward.
Spaniards survey the scene in serious mode.
Indian nurses are here with all the courtesies of
the Raj.

Where are all the English nurses, and the Irish too?
Fifty years ago, a junior doctor was I.
English nurses and Irish too were there,
But where have the English nurses gone?

English nurses the world admires,
Indeed, the world has come
To join the English nurses,
But they've mostly gone.

RELIGION

28. Love and Death

The great command of Jesus,
Was that one another we should love,
As He loved us,
Yet the great love that Jesus in his life did show,
To all who came to Him,
Did not prevent the people's cry:
Crucify Him, Crucify Him.

So, does love always love beget?
Sadly, it is not always so.
A loving act much hatred may receive.
Death from human kindness may result.
It ever has been so.

Love's greatest expression,
Our Lord did say,
Were our lives to give away
For friends.
Then love and death
May embrace and intertwine.

The human heart when great love doth bear,
Great pain may suffer too,
When the beloved cannot such passion match.
Love without hope may onwards lead,
To painful melancholy and death.

Yet when loving deed is done,
We must hope and pray,
That those who see such love shine forth,
From love to hate my turn,
And thoughts of death may fade away.

29. Thou

Thou didst leave Thy throne,
For the unlikely likes of me,
So, for many today,
It is You they address,
In a quite informal way.
But a way that is loving too.
Yet for me I find the Lordship real,
And there is no other way.
In the kitchen too, sitting with me,
It is Thou I see,
Not an ordinary man in a dungaree.

30. Triumph

Christians believe the path of Love
Is the way to go.
Eckists too, as they chant the Hu,
Follow this way of life.
At this time, when darkness and hate
Across the world do spread,
Time it is,
For those who follow this path
To remember
Love will triumph one day.

31. Martyr Bishop

Wandering in Merton College Chapel,
I came upon
A memorial,
With an image
Long familiar from my childhood,
In distant Sydney,
Within St Giles's church.
In my memory,
In stained glass window,
Bishop Coleridge Patteson's
Young face shines forth,
Brilliantly illuminated
By southern sun.
He stood,
In Bishop's robes
With hand upon the head
Of youthful Melanesian.
He and Saint Paul flanked the image
Of our Lord,
Bedecked with crown of thorns.

O youthful gentle Bishop,
Martyred for your faith
In Nukapau,
It is recorded,
A South Pacific isle,
So far from home.
Here, in Merton's sacred shrine,
You are yet remembered still
As one who gave his life
For those he chose to serve,
As did our Lord.

32. A Priest Now

Before the people,
Tall and radiant he stood.
Many hands had lain upon his head.
Two thousand years stretched back,
To Christ Himself.

Bending low in surplice white,
With golden stole,
He laid his hands upon the bended heads,
Of those before him kneeling,
Humbly whispering God's blessing.

God is here, she said.
Today God reveals Himself,
In the lives of those who follow Him.
Today we saw God's hand
Laid on those seeking Him.

33. Chapel of the Savoy

Founded by Peter of Savoy,
John of Gaunt a great palace built.
Destroyed by peasants in revolt.
All that survives is the chapel,
Now a chapel of the King,
A Chapel Royal no less.

Through tumultuous centuries despite fires and
Nazi bombs.
The chapel stands, a sacred place of serenity and
peace.
The singing of the chapel by choir and people sounds
forth,
With the ethereal tones of the boy choristers rising
heavenwards.
It remains an oasis of calm in a time of perpetual
discord and decay.
But there is no despair; rather, here, hope is found,
The sure and certain hope of the resurrection of the
dead,
And the life of the world to come.

POETRY

34. The Poet

On the occasion of meeting Stephen Spender
1985

Meeting you was brief and short,
Yet as you looked at me,
Did you discern a soul,
Touched by your youthful words and deeds,
So long ago?
White-haired and tall you stood,
One whose inner life you shared with all.
Your momentary look
Still remains with me.
Friends we could have been,
Despite an age gap of nigh forty years,
But never would we meet again,
I sadly thought,
As I reluctantly away did wander.

ROYALTY

35. The Queen

I did but see her passing by,
But I did see her more,
I was to shake her hand one day.
She with furrowed brow did break.
Diarrhoea in children, what can this be?
In front of her to mention such,
Unwise might thought to be,
But she who just the same,
Those two imposters treats,
Moved on with a determined smile.

36. Trooping the Colour 2006

I did but see them passing by,
As down the Mall walked I.
Purple hat and black bearskin
As Queen and Duke
Slowly glided by.

Amidst the pomp and pride
Of Britain's cavalry and guards,
A serene image of
Sincerity and quiet duty
Provided they.

No spin is theirs,
No political correctness,
Just a little human kindness,
And dignity,
In a world of cynicism,
And restlessness.

37. Cynicism

Cynicism, cynicism,
How I hate the word.
The media do love it,
It is their greatest joy.
But large "rewards" do come,
When you tear down the mighty,
Royalty especially, as Diana knew so well.
Yet do they really want
All illusion to shatter?
When a mirror breaks,
The viewer is shattered too.

38. Thank You, Ma'am

A Eulogy for Queen Elizabeth

Grief and love,
She linked them so.
Comfortable words:
But power from words may flow,
And fill our hearts with love.

From Edinburgh to Sydney,
From London to Ottawa,
And more,
This loss doth flow,
Right across
The world we know.
All have mothers,
Mama, *Mum*,
Mom and more!
Was she mother of us all?
Who can say? But, in our loss,
Love remains,
Darkly it may seem,
But on another shore,
It is our hope,
She will then be known,
Face to face,
As we have known her here.

TRAVEL AND PLACES

39. First Glimpse of Home

From earliest memories,
My mother had told me tales of a "Home".
Where she had never been.
From earliest memories,
It was homeward I sought to go,
And to see my land of dreams.

After six and twenty years,
As a ship's surgeon,
I did come "home".
Young, free and romantic was I.
Often, I dreamt
Of that land of tales and hopes, unknown,
That green and pleasant land,
Oft sung in Chapel, long ago.
So, when we at last approached her,
And I saw those cliffs so white,
With swards so green upon them,
It was almost too much for me.

40. England

Those lush green fields,
I longed to see,
They filled my thoughts,
And stole my heart away,
Though never seen by me.

O land of my ancestors,
So very far away,
Why should I think of thee?

The lusty brown land of my birth,
Surrounded by a tumultuous sea,
Did much appeal to me,
Yet far away, in Northern climes,
Lay the land where I wanted to be.

I yearned for the land of lush green fields,
Of gentle folk and quiet serenity,
Where I might kind friends find,
Then we could wander the hills and downs
And find such peace and joy.

Now I have walked the Downs,
Close by Seaford's tall head,
And near the dreaming spires,
Yet still I yearn for peace and joy,
Which I hope may yet to be.

41. In Paradisum

Kyrie Eleison
Rose up from far below,
Grandson and I,
Stood in gallery high,
So close to the golden vault
Of San Marco's church.
As those ethereal tones,
Our hearts did touch.
Above the arch of Paradise, we stood.

Then to our left we turned,
And in a quiet corner
The four horses did we see,
Bronze, gilded with gold,
But alive,
And with joy, prancing.
Were they startled
From their ancient reverie
By the sweet music of paradise,
So far below?

For a moment,
The beauty of sound
And sight,
Together,
Had given us both
A glimpse of Heaven.

42. Byron in Venezia

Our vaporetto
A palace passed,
Upon whose wall
A white plaque did gleam.
A brash American dad
Informed his son,
"That's where Lord Byron,
The pirate, lived."

As on we went,
Lido-bound,
I reflected that Byron
From thence had swum.
At first, Palazzo Ducale
Bound was he,
But onwards,
To Canal Grande's end,
Had he swum.

Mad, bad,
Perhaps.
Dangerous to know,
Perhaps,
But no pirate
He!

43. A Doctor Reflects after Visiting Auschwitz 2009

Mengele,
Torturer of children,
In the name of medicine!

To mourn?
It is not enough!
To rage?
Is it more?
To hope?
Yes, we must.

Yes,
I do know,
You were there.
As well,
As all in all,
Everywhere.

But please, O Lord
Why, why, why,
Could such things be?

FRIENDSHIP AND LOVE

44. So Many Loves

Love for family, love for home,
Love for she who gave us
Bairns to love and cherish so.
Love for friends and those close to heart,
Love for country; on it goes.
There are so may loves!
But the greatest love,
Is the love of those,
Who give their lives for friends.

45. A Pure Heart

See that ye love one another,
With a pure heart fervently,
We choir boys sang,
With a purity of tone
That matched the thought,
As bride and bridegroom,
Before the altar stood,
In quiet simplicity.

Before had entered
Into our hearts
The pangs of love
And thoughts of death,
Fervently we sang,
Alert to the beauty of the scene,
Pregnant with hope,
Of happiness to come.

Cynics claim, such choirboys
Never can innocent be.
Yet our hearts were filled with a purity,
Of hope for love that was to be.

Years have passed,
Yet soprano voices
Singing fervently
Now stir my memory,
And sadness fills my heart.
I fear I have not fulfilled,
The hope in me entrusted
On another wedding day.
It was too hard for me.

46. Airport 1

Too late, too late,
I discovered the love
For me you bore.
My cup was overflowing,
My love was even more.
But the tyranny of time,
And the need to journey on
Defeated us together.
Yet the memory was forever,
And has been for ever more.

47. Two Candles

Two candles
Lit in St Paul's
Side by side they stand,
Within the bowl of sand.
Their flames burn
Bright and true,
As tokens of loving friendship
Newly found.

Slowly they slide together,
The flames becoming one.
It burns brighter still
And upwards soars,
By chance is this,
Or is it a higher power,
Giving signal clear,
To him who stands and watches?

May two friends' love,
Each for each,
Long endure,
In endless amity.

48. You

How much I have loved you,
I alone do know.
Perhaps it is too much for you
And might irk you so.

So, for you,
No symmetry of love
Can ever be.

Yet friendship is for ever.
That is my hope,
For you,
For me.

49. Together Then

In your country again,
But you are not with me.
It can be hard to bear,
But I soldier on.
You are happy and not alone.
This comforts me.

But the years that are gone,
They were great for me,
When we were
Together, then.

Walking along the lakeside,
Climbing the mountains green,
In the summer sun,
In the evenings too,
Times to remember forever,
When we were
Together, then.

50. Words

I love you,
Say I.
It is just words,
You say.
This cannot be so!

I know,
You reciprocate not.
This is clear.
But words of love,
Are rich and rare,
To dismiss my words
Is hard to bear.

My love is deep and true,
You wound me.
But why is not clear to me.
Love is not lust.
You seem not to understand.
Love is a gift.
Reject it not.
Turn not away from me.

51. The Rainbow

How much I have loved you.
I alone do know.

Too much for you,
It irks you so.

Yet love unreturned
Its own rainbow doth have.

Or so I have been told.
And so, for me, it is true.

There is a joy in the giving,
And I offer my joy
In my love for you.

52. Now

Back in your country with you
Now.
But it is another country
Now.
We are not together
Now.
But joy and love remain
Now.
Such loving friendship is forever and
Now.

53. The Photographs

How they remind me of you,
Remembering your voice,
Walking alone with you.
Winter and summer too,
With gentle spring and autumn warmth.
Fragment of memory,
Mountains, snow,
Swimming in summer lake.

Wonderful welcome,
Heartfelt parting.

My black hair, now white,
Now glasses too.
But photos take me back,
To our halcyon days.

Memories open,
Memories with you,
To remember the joy
We had together,
And now return.

54. A Troubled Friend

When a friend is troubled,
You are troubled too.
'Tis hard to know just what to do.
But stand by him
And let him know,
"I am here for you!"

No man is an island,
But we wander alone.

There are fellows who help,
There are those who but hinder,

But friends together,
Stand shoulder to shoulder,
Hand in hand,
To defy those who stare.

A friend will give you a boost,
Nudge you along.
Others, so busy
With the ways of the world,
Have no time to spare
At all.

But friends are forever.
They find a way,
Together they stand,
In defiant resolve,
Till the troubles dissolve.

Then onward they go,
Not alone, but together
Contra mundum.

MYSELF

55. Don't Cry, John

Don't cry, John,
My mother said,
The day my dog died.
Boys don't cry, John.

My father did not cry
The day my mother died.
For him, it was clear,
Men do not cry, John!

When my daughter,
Then my nephew died,
I could do naught
But cry.

Times change,
Customs come and go.
Now even footballers cry in victory and defeat!

56. Outsider Boy

He is not like other boys,
His dad said.
What does that mean?
He said in his head.

Ham handed, is he,
Said his dad,
So true, said he,
In his head.

Cricket, I hate,
I am always too late
To catch the ball,
He said in his head.

But rugby is good,
He can tackle okay,
Said his dad,
Well that is good,
He said in his head.

57. Trapped

Trapped,
Trapped,
In words am I.

Good intentions
Good intentions!
But what do they mean

When the evil ones
The words
Do twist and spin?

How long, O Lord,
How long, I cry,
Till it will end?

But, Kafka, Kafka,
Am I trapped with you?
How will it end?

DOGS

58. Your Dog and You

I saw you together,
Your dog and you
Walking in the woods,
Swimming in the pool.

Love and loyalty
Is your dog's gift to you,
A gift I could see.
You respond in kind.

Loyalty and love:
Treasures for Heaven,
Given to us by dogs, a lesson for all to see,
Your dog and you.

59. Your Dog Has Gone

Years have passed
For your dog and you.
To you, his all was given.
But he has gone.

The shades have lengthened,
The evening has come.
But he gave love to you.
Dogs teach us to value friends.
He was indeed a friend to you.

THE PANDEMIC

60. Good Friday at a Time of Corona

He died upon the Cross
A sacrifice for love, for all,
Limitless love,
Across time and space.

Laying down life,
For friends
No greater love there is,
We're told.

Since Corona came to slay us,
Many their lives
Have cruelly lost,
Serving strangers
They did not know.

In this land, doctors, nurses
And others too,
Have made the sacrifice, supreme,
As their forbears did in time of war,
Dark times, so long ago.

As Christ did, upon the cross,
So cruelly die,
His breath did fail.
Cruel Corona, too,
Steals the breath away.

But those who Jesus love,
Who die today,
Today will see Him too.

For from the Cross
He said,
You will be with me
In paradise, today.

61. My Daughter Now

A cornucopia of life has flowed from you.
Blessings six have come.
On your wedding day, your eyes looked out
To a bright and fertile future with
The one you love.
So it has proved to be.
And your life is rich,
With love in action.

Born in a sunny land,
You have brought sun and comfort too
For those in need.

For me with the shadow of Corona,
You have shielded me,
And circled my life with shining,
As I felt on your wedding day.

Inspired by the poem 'To My Daughter'
by Stephen Spender, which I quoted in my
speech at my daughter's wedding day.

62. Christmas at a Time of Corona

Not isolated, but alone at home,
I have the Zoom and the phone,
For family near and far, but still alone.
But Lexie with me, can still in forest roam.

The joy of Christmas past is with me still,
Its memory fast, with much love,
For love it is, at Christmas's heart.
Such love will never fade.

Holly and ivy,
Thorns and blood,
Tell you that even with joy,
Sorrow may not be far away.

So, sorrows too many, with time, may
By joy be overtaken,
As Easter follows Good Friday.

The joy of family at Christmas,
As of old, will return.
But when? I hope 'tis soon,
Is what I say.

63. Deliver Us from Evil in a Time of Corona

Deliver us from evil, we pray each livelong day.
Deliver us from plague, did our forebears say.
Corona too, in its evil way, may slay us too.

Why do these evil diseases come?
You hear men say.
But scientists say, *know, we do not.*

But other evils there are today.
Electronic evil may seek our souls to slay.
Evil mails are there to peace destroy.

We do know from whence they come,
From fellow humans with cruel hearts.
The power of evil they do display,
Causing pain and misery,
Sin is not far away.

Yet God is there.
He will not fail to pardon sin,
To deliver us from evil,
From Corona fear and cruel humans too.
Love will triumph in the end.

64. A Friend at a Time of Corona

A wise man said, four loves there be.
Friendship is one of these.
At Corona's dark time, if aged you be,
Shielded must be your fate.
Daughter dear showed her love,
Shielding me.

But then you appeared,
To assist me, a library to build,
'Twas the task.
Many were the books we counted,
A thousand and more, much more.
And friend you soon became.

You brought me joy and laughter,
Enriched my life.
We talked of lands and times past,
That my books revealed,
Visited in times so long gone.

Then in the blink of an eye, you were gone.
Parting was so very hard.
How right the wise man way!
It is my dearest wish,
Come the day,
When we shall meet again.

METAPHYSICS

65. Roman Glass

A Roman made me,
Earth sustained me,
The sun displays me,
Time creates me.
Iridescent am I,
Beauty on display.
Man, and nature, created me,
Nigh two thousand years.
Ephemeral am I?
None can know,
But do you glimpse the eternal through me?
Will I last forever?

From man and nature in harmony
Much beauty may arise.
And you emerge.
Transcendent beauty?
Iridescence
Transcendence
The same essence?
Truth is beauty and beauty is truth
Saith the poet.

I do affirm.
In my colours bright,
In the glare of the sun,
Mankind and Creator together.

66. The Colour Blue

The cloth of heaven is blue,
'Tis true.
The ark with cloth of blue,
Was covered,
And shewbread too,
Lay upon a cloth of blue, the coolest of colours.
Artists, too,
Painted Mary wearing the colour blue.
Is it a holy hue?

The ever-changing sea,
Moves from light to dark blue,
In its restless moodiness,
From summer's brightness
To winter's shadows.

But does blue in sea, sky or land transcend?
Does blue speak to us?
Of another world, a transcendent world,
A world of beauty,
Where deeper things
Do last for ever and for ever?